# THE ELEMENTS

## Boron

# Richard Beatty

**Marshall Cavendish**
Benchmark

New York

Marshall Cavendish Benchmark
99 White Plains Road
Tarrytown, New York 10591

www.marshallcavendish.us

Library of Congress Cataloging-in-Publication Data

Beatty, Richard.
Boron / by Richard Beatty.
p.      cm. — (Elements)
Includes index
ISBN-13 978-0-7614-1921-1
ISBN 0-7614-1921-7
1. Boron—Juvenile literature. I. Title. II. Elements (Marshall
Cavendish Benchmark)
QD181.B1B47 2005
546'.671—dc22

2005042159

6 5 4 3 2

Printed in China

**Picture credits**
Front Cover: Corbis, Lester V. Bergman
Back Cover: Corbis, Richard Cummins

Stan Celestian: 11
Corbis: James L. Amos 19, Lester V. Bergman 4, 5, 6, Richard Cummins 7,
Aaron Horowitz 3, 14, Charles O'Rear 25, Galen Rowell 10, 20
Image State: 1, 22
Tom Jackson: 24
Photos.com: 26, 27, 30
Science Photo Library: Ben Johnson 12, 16, Lawrence Livermore National Laboratory 23
University of Pennsylvania Library: Edgar Fahs Smith Collection 9

Series created by The Brown Reference Group plc.
Designed by Sarah Williams
www.brownreference.com

# Contents

# What is boron?

Boron is an important industrial chemical element, and one that also has an interesting history. People have been using boron-containing substances since written history began. However, scientists did not discover the element itself until the early nineteenth century.

Scientists describe pure boron as a metalloid, or semimetal. Although it is shiny and hard like a metal, it does not

| BORON FACTS | |
|---|---|
| ● Chemical symbol: | B |
| ● Atomic number: | 5 |
| ● Atomic mass number: | 10 or 11 (average 10.81) |
| ● Density: | 2.36 grams in every cubic cm. (2.36 times denser than water.) |
| ● Melting point: | 2300 °C (4170 °F) |
| ● Boiling point: | 2550 °C (4620 °F) |

(These figures are for amorphous boron. Crystalline boron has different melting and boiling points.)

conduct electricity well. Boron combines with other elements to form compounds (substances that contain atoms of two or more elements). Many of these compounds are unusual because the atoms are joined into chains or rings. Boron compounds have many uses, ranging from glassmaking to agriculture. Some of the hardest and toughest materials in the world are boron compounds.

*There are two forms of boron. Crystalline boron, shown here, is a shiny black solid. Amorphous boron (a form that does not have a repeating crystal structure) is a brown powder.*

## Borax

The most important boron substance found in nature is called borax. In ancient times, borax was a rare and precious material. The merchants who traded it kept their borax sources a secret. However, most of it seems to have come from remote salt lakes hidden in the mountains of Tibet.

From the mid-1800s onward, deposits of boron compounds were discovered in Death Valley, California, and elsewhere in the western United States. Up to twenty mules would haul several wagons packed with borax across the desert. These so-called mule trains soon became famous. Pictures of the wagons were used to advertise boron-containing products, such as soaps and laundry powders.

*Borax is a shiny white crystal. It is the most common boron compound and also contains sodium and oxygen atoms.*

## The boron atom

Like other elements, boron consists of tiny atoms. Every atom has a small but heavy nucleus in the center. The nucleus has a positive charge. Negatively charged particles called electrons orbit the nucleus. Opposite charges attract, so the negative electrons stay close to the positive nucleus. The nucleus gets its positive charge from particles inside it called protons. A proton is many times larger and heavier than an electron. The number of electrons in an atom is always the same as the number of protons. The electrons and protons cancel out each other's charges so that the atom has no overall charge—it is neutral.

The number of protons in an atom's nucleus is called the atomic number. This number is unique to each element. Since a boron atom has five protons, its atomic number is five.

The nucleus of most atoms, including boron's, also contains other particles that are just slightly heavier than protons. These particles have no charge. Since they are neutral, the particles are called neutrons. The number of an atom's protons and neutrons is the atomic mass number.

Boron atoms come in two forms, or isotopes. Each isotope has a different number of neutrons, and therefore a different atomic mass number. One isotope contains five neutrons in the nucleus: it is called boron-10 (with five protons and five neutrons). About four-fifths of all boron atoms are the boron-11 isotope. These have six neutrons in their nucleus.

## Boron as a substance

Pure boron exists either as amorphous boron, which is a brown powder, or crystalline boron, which is a hard shiny black crystal. In boron crystals, the atoms are packed together in a complex three-dimensional arrangement, though this is far too small to see with the eye. Boron crystals are extremely hard, but they are too brittle (easily broken) to be useful materials on their own. Boron only reacts with other chemicals when it is hot. At cool temperatures it is very stable.

*Borax powder is sprinkled on the seams of a steel bowl. The borax will help fuse the metal together when the bowl is heated in a fire.*

## BORON ATOM

**First shell**

**Second shell**

**Nucleus**

The number of positively charged protons in the nucleus of an atom is balanced by the number of negatively charged particles, called electrons, outside the nucleus. A boron atom contains 5 electrons. These orbit the nucleus in two layers, or shells. There are 2 electrons in the inner shell and 3 in the outer shell.

# The history of boron

*A train of wagons at the Harmony Borax Works in Death Valley, California. The train was loaded with borax and pulled across the desert by 20 mules.*

People have probably used naturally occurring borax for thousands of years, even though pure boron was not discovered until 1808. The word *borax* has a long history. It goes back more than 600 years in English, and versions of the word in Arabic and Persian are even older. However, the term was used for other boron compounds as well, and it is not always clear if early writers are talking about borax as it is known today.

## Changing uses

The world's first civilizations in China and the Middle East used borax for various purposes, even though it was rare and difficult to get hold of. Goldsmiths and silversmiths melted borax and used it as a flux. A flux is a substance that removes unwanted impurities from metals. Ever since then potters have been using borax in glazes (surface coatings) for clay pots. Borax-containing skin ointments were also widely used, until recently.

The craftspeople of Europe continued to use borax in the same way until at least the late eighteenth century. In the nineteenth century, new sources of borax were discovered. As a result, boron became much less expensive.

At this time scientists began to study the chemistry of boron compounds, and people began looking for new ways to use borax. For example, the substance was added to soap to boost its cleaning abilities. In 1875, Joseph Lister (1827–1912), a famous British surgeon, used borax as an antiseptic (a substance that kills germs).

By 1900, the single biggest use of boron compounds was in making hard enamel coverings for metal objects, such as stoves and pots. Later on, more boron began to be used by the glassmaking industry. This industry is still the largest user of boron compounds today.

The modern chemical industry also made use of very pure boron. Today pure boron and its compounds are used in many ways. They are added to fertilizers, they make objects ultra-hard or fireproof, and pure boron is even used to control nuclear reactions.

## DISCOVERERS

### HUMPHRY DAVY

The scientist and inventor Humphry Davy was born in 1778 in Cornwall, in southwest England. In his research, Davy used electric batteries, which had just been invented. Davy extracted metals from minerals by melting them and passing electricity through the liquid. As a result, he discovered sodium, potassium, calcium, magnesium, and boron. Davy named boron after borax, but this was not his first name for the new element. At first he thought boron was a metal and gave it a metallic-sounding name: boracium. By 1812 he realized that the element was more like carbon, and changed its name to *boron*.

Boron was also isolated around the same time as Davy by two French chemists working together, Joseph-Louis Thenard and Louis-Jacques Gay-Lussac. The French scientists often quarreled with Davy over who had discovered boron and several other elements.

## Exploration and trade

By the year 1500, the valuable trade bringing borax from Asia to Europe was controlled by the city of Venice in Italy, which was a great trading power. Later on, the Dutch controlled the trade. Then, around 1827, a new European source of supply became available—natural boric acid [$B(OH_3)$] from hot springs in Italy.

Deposits of boron minerals were first mined in the deserts of California and Nevada in the 1860s. Before long a "borax rush" began, with many miners traveling to the area hoping to get rich by digging

for borax. The United States soon became the world's biggest supplier of boron compounds, using sources in the Mojave Desert, Death Valley, and elsewhere.

For more than forty years until 1925, the world's most important boron mineral was colemanite. This was named for U.S. businessman William T. Coleman, who owned the world's main source at a boron mine in Death Valley.

In 1925, huge underground deposits of another boron mineral, kernite, were found near what is now the town of Boron, California. Today, the mine at

Boron is the world's biggest. However a lot of boron is also mined in Turkey, Argentina, and other countries.

## Scientific advances

In the late 1700s, scientists began to wonder if borax and boric acid contained a new, undiscovered element. All efforts to isolate the new element failed. Eventually, in 1808, an impure form of boron was produced by English chemist Humphry Davy (1778–1829) and by French chemists

*Humphry Davy discovered boron and several other elements, but he is best known for inventing a miner's safety lamp. The lamp had a grill that prevented the flame inside from causing explosions.*

Joseph-Louis Gay-Lussac (1778 –1850) and Louis-Jacques Thenard (1777–1857) in France. Both Davy and the French scientists obtained boron by reacting borates (compounds containing boron and oxygen) with potassium metal. (Davy had discovered potassium the previous year.)

# Where boron is found

In the universe as a whole, boron is a rare element. Boron atoms only form in unusual circumstances. Scientists think that the processes that created different chemical elements inside large stars do not generally produce much boron. However, some boron is found in moon rocks and in meteorites falling to Earth from space.

## Boron on Earth

Boron is never found in a pure, uncombined state on Earth. There are more than 200 different natural boron compounds. Natural compounds are called minerals. Most of the boron minerals are borates. Boron compounds tend to be soluble, which means they can dissolve in water. Boron is more common near the Earth's surface because the compounds have been carried up from deep rocks by hot underground water. The sea also contains dissolved boron compounds.

## Commercial sources

Some parts of the world, such as California, have large deposits of boron-containing minerals. Over a long time, water with boron compounds in it floods into low-lying areas. The water evaporates in the

*The Mojave Desert in southern California contains some of the world's largest deposits of boron minerals, such as borax and kernite.*

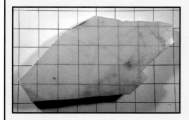
dry conditions, leaving the boron compounds behind. Eventually thick layers of white borate crystals pile up. These are usually in desert regions where there has also been volcanic activity.

Boron minerals contain a range of metals. Some also have water molecules locked inside of their crystals. The amount of water inside the minerals also varies widely. For example, when borax is buried deep underground, it changes into a different mineral called kernite. The heat and pressure under the ground drives water out of the borax crystals making them kernite. A more unusual kind of boron mineral, found especially in Italy, is made of solid boric acid. This is found around the edges of hot springs.

# Mining and refining

Mining boron is a huge industry, but just a few countries have large enough deposits of boron ore to make it worthwhile to mine it. (An ore is any rock or mineral that is valuable enough to be worth mining.) California and Turkey are the world's two highest producers.

## Extracting the ore

Most boron ores are extracted by the open-pit method rather than by digging underground tunnels. Miners using the pit method need to remove a large quantity of unwanted rocks on top of the ore. The ore is then loosened by explosives, gathered

---

**DID YOU KNOW?**

Added together many countries produce a total of 5,070,000 tons (4,600,000 tonnes) of pure boron oxide ($B_2O_3$), the most useful boron compound.

| Country | Tonnage |
| --- | --- |
| Turkey | 1,540,000 tons (1,400,000 tonnes) |
| United States | 1,300,000 tons (1,180,000 tonnes) |
| Russia | 1,100,000 tons (1,000,000 tonnes) |
| Argentina | 400,000 tons (360,000 tonnes) |
| Chile | 375,000 tons (340,000 tonnes) |
| China | 120,000 tons (110,000 tonnes) |

---

*Kernite is a boron-containing mineral that is very similar to borax. The world's largest supply of kernite is from Boron, California. This town was named for its huge mine.*

up by huge diggers, and placed in massive dump trucks that carry it away. A huge hole, or pit, is left in the ground where the ore used to be.

The ore is turned into pure boron at a complex called a refinery. The refinery is generally close to the pit so the ore does not have to be moved far.

## Refining

Most boron ores are borates. Borax, for example, is a type of sodium borate ($Na_2B_4O_7$). Pure boron has to be separated from the other elements in the ore by several chemical reactions. However, many boron ores are useful substances on their own and do not need to be purified by a chemical process. Instead, refineries wash away the impurities with water.

Hot water is added first to dissolve the borate and leave the sand, grit, and other dirt behind. Large bits of these impurities are filtered out through a fine sievelike grill. Then this borate solution (a liquid with borate dissolved in it) is left to stand. This allows smaller unwanted particles, such as clay, to sink to the bottom.

The cleaned borate solution is then cooled down. This causes the borate to form solid crystals. The crystals are dried before being used. One of the main uses of purified borax, for example, is to make boric acid, another useful boron-containing compound.

## Pure boron

Several different methods are used to obtain pure boron. The main method involves three chemical reactions. (A chemical reaction occurs when atoms of different elements recombine into different compounds.) First, purified

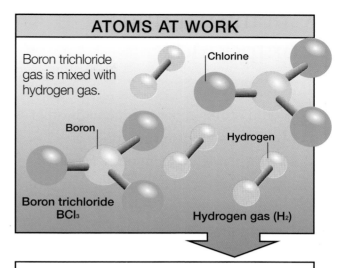

## ATOMS AT WORK

Boron trichloride gas is mixed with hydrogen gas.

Chlorine

Boron

Hydrogen

Boron trichloride $BCl_3$

Hydrogen gas ($H_2$)

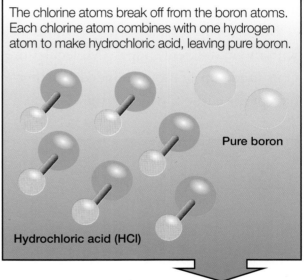

The chlorine atoms break off from the boron atoms. Each chlorine atom combines with one hydrogen atom to make hydrochloric acid, leaving pure boron.

Pure boron

Hydrochloric acid (HCl)

The reaction that takes place can be written like this:

$$2BCl_3 + 3H_2 \rightarrow 2B + 6HCl$$

borax or another borate mineral is made into boron carbide gas ($B_4C$). This gas is reacted with chlorine gas to make boron trichloride gas. The boron trichloride gas is then mixed with hydrogen gas to make pure boron and hydrochloric acid.

# Chemistry and compounds

Boron atoms can combine with other elements to form thousands of different chemical compounds. Many of them are very useful and used in industry. But compared to most elements, the chemistry of boron is unusual. For years, chemists were baffled by the structure of many boron compounds.

Boron forms a wide variety of molecules with many different shapes. (Molecules are units made up of atoms bonded together.) Except for carbon, which is the element that makes up most of the bodies of living things, boron probably has the most complicated chemistry of all the elements.

## The chemistry of boron

Atoms form bonds with each other in two main ways. Both ways involve the atoms' electrons. An atom's electrons move around the nucleus in layered shells. Just the electrons in the outer shell are involved in forming chemical bonds. Whether an atom bonds to another is decided by how many outer electrons each one has.

*A boric acid crystal magnified 100 times. The crystal has been cut into a very thin strip.*

Many elements form bonds by moving some of their outer electrons to the atom of another element. This makes the first atom positively charged and gives the second a negative charge. The two atoms are then held together because their opposite charges attract each other. Atoms that lose or gain electrons are called ions. Bonds between ions are described as ionic.

Boron does not form ionic bonds. Too much energy is needed to take a boron atom's electrons away, and boron atoms are not good at pulling electrons off other atoms. Instead boron bonds by sharing electrons with other atoms. This is called covalent bonding.

A simple covalent bond froms between two atoms and involves two electrons, one coming from each atom. Boron has three outermost electrons, and so usually forms three covalent bonds. It can also form a fourth bond, but only if the other atom provides both electrons for the bond.

## Electron-deficient bonds

Boron also forms unusual covalent bonds using fewer electrons than usual. In some boron compounds a single pair of electrons are shared between three atoms, not two. Compounds like this are described as electron-deficient. Scientists were so puzzled when they discovered these unusual boron compounds that they had to create a whole new theory to explain how they worked.

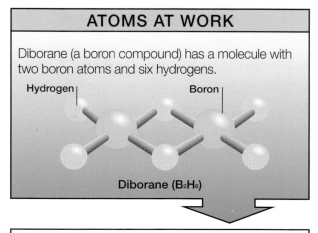

### ATOMS AT WORK

Diborane (a boron compound) has a molecule with two boron atoms and six hydrogens.

Hydrogen | Boron |

Diborane ($B_2H_6$)

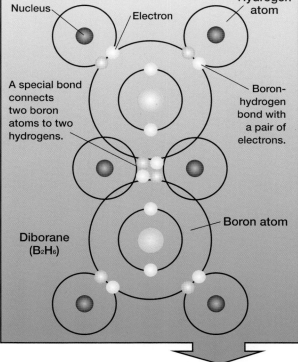

Most of the bonds between the hydrogen and boron atoms involve two electrons. Each atom donates one electron to the pair. However, the two central hydrogen atoms are each joined to both of the boron atoms because there are not enough electrons to pair up into four normal bonds. Therefore the two central hydrogen atoms share two pairs of electrons with the two boron atoms.

Nucleus

Electron

Hydrogen atom

A special bond connects two boron atoms to two hydrogens.

Boron–hydrogen bond with a pair of electrons.

Diborane ($B_2H_6$)

Boron atom

Diborane is an example of an electron-deficient compound. It has the formula $B_2H_6$.

Therefore, boron atoms can form several bonds each, either with other boron atoms or with other elements. The crystals of boron compounds have very intricate structures. Many contain long chains or networks of atoms. Others are filled with ball-like shapes made up of twelve atoms linked together.

## Borax and borates

Most naturally occurring boron exists in the form of borates. Borates are compounds of boron and oxygen that also contain metal atoms. The most important of them are the sodium borates. These compounds all have a similar chemistry. The main difference between them is the amount of water included in their crystals. Heating can change one kind of sodium borate to another by removing some of the water.

The name *borax* is often used for any of these sodium borates. Strictly speaking, however, borax is one particular compound that includes ten water molecules in its crystal structure. Its full chemical name is sodium tetraborate decahydrate ($Na_2B_4O_7.10H_2O$).

## Boric acid

Boric acid is an important industrial compound. It is made in factories by adding sulfuric acid to borate minerals. Boric acid is a solid at room temperature and consists of small molecules with the formula $B(OH)_3$. Boric acid is a very weak acid. It can be used to kill insects and other small animals, but its main importance is in making other boron compounds. For this, it is usually converted to boron oxide first. This is done by heating the solid acid to drive off water molecules.

*A sample of colemanite, a boron-containing mineral found in Death Valley, California. Colemanite also contains calcium and oxygen atoms.*

## ATOMS AT WORK

Boric oxide is made by heating boric acid.

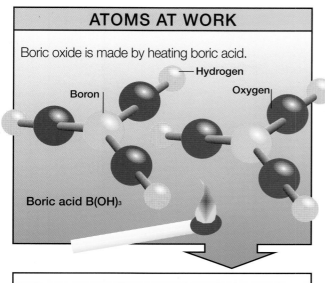

Boron

Hydrogen

Oxygen

Boric acid B(OH)₃

The heat makes the hydrogen atoms and some of the oxygen ones split from the boron compound.

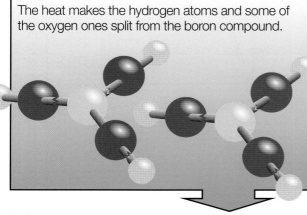

These hydrogen and oxygen atoms combine to form water vapor. The remaining boron and oxygen atoms join together to make boric oxide crystals.

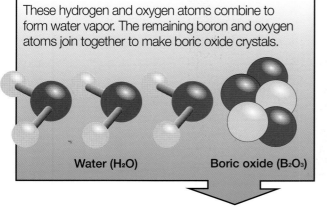

Water (H₂O)          Boric oxide (B₂O₃)

The reaction that takes place can be written like this:

**2B(OH)₃ → B₂O₃ + 3H₂O**

## Metal borides

Borides are compounds that have boron combined with a metal and nothing else. Zinc, titanium, and chromium borides are probably the most important for industrial processes. However, many other borides are made. Some borides, such as titanium diboride ($TiB_2$), contain more boron atoms than metal atoms. Others have more metal atoms than boron ones.

Borides are extremely hard and melt at very high temperatures. Although expensive to make, borides are used in heat-resistant materials.

## Nitride and carbide

Boron nitride and carbide compounds are the two hardest substances known after diamond. Both of these boron compounds have important uses (see page 23).

Boron nitride is the harder of the two and has the formula BN. Many of its properties relate to the fact that boron and nitrogen are similar to carbon atoms. Boron nitride can exist in two different forms that are very similar to the two main forms of carbon—diamond and graphite. (Graphite is used as pencil lead.)

The hard, diamond-like form of boron nitride is called cubic boron nitride. The softer form, called hexagonal boron nitride, has its molecules arranged into sheets. This gives it slippery properties similar to graphite's.

Boron carbide is cheaper to produce than boron nitride, but it is a more reactive compound. It has a complex crystal structure with a formula that is either $B_4C$ or $B_6C$. However, a crystal of boron carbide may have up to 13 boron atoms for every two carbon ones.

## Other boron compounds

Compounds of boron and hydrogen are called boranes. German chemist Alfred Stock (1876–1946) was the first to study these. His work led to the discovery of electron-deficient compounds.

A huge number of boranes can be made, each with a different geometrical shape. Many are liquids or gases at room temperature. The simplest, diborane, has the formula $B_2H_6$. Boranes also form compounds with metals. Sodium borohydride ($NaBH_4$) is used for bleaching wood pulp.

In the 1950s there was great excitement among the U.S. military that boranes might be the jet fuel of the future, because they weigh less than normal fuels. Millions of dollars were spent on research and development, but boranes proved too difficult and dangerous to work with.

Boron trichloride ($BCl_3$) is another important boron compound. It is made industrially by combining chlorine with boron carbide. Boron trichloride is used for making pure boron.

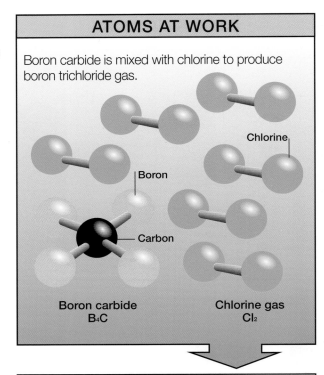

## ATOMS AT WORK

Boron carbide is mixed with chlorine to produce boron trichloride gas.

Chlorine

Boron

Carbon

Boron carbide
$B_4C$

Chlorine gas
$Cl_2$

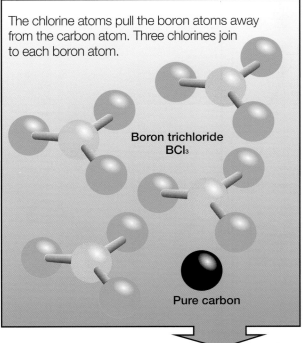

The chlorine atoms pull the boron atoms away from the carbon atom. Three chlorines join to each boron atom.

Boron trichloride
$BCl_3$

Pure carbon

The reaction that takes place can be written like this:

$$B_4C + 6Cl_2 \rightarrow C + 4BCl_3$$

# Uses of boron

*A glassmaker heats a Pyrex tube. This type of glass is made with boron compounds. It is used to make cooking dishes and laboratory equipment.*

Natural boron minerals have been used as ingredients for a range of products for many years. Other boron compounds have only been made using modern chemistry. Boron compounds are useful for several reasons. They are very hard, resistant to heat, and also have an effect on living things.

## Glass and pottery

Today, the glassmaking industry is the biggest single user of boron compounds. It uses more than half of the total world production. Glass is an unusual type of solid because its molecules are not arranged in repeating rows. Instead, they are arranged in a random order. This makes them hard and smooth, but also likely to shatter. The main ingredient of glass is silica (silicon dioxide, found naturally in sand). To make glass, silica is combined with other substances to create silicon and oxygen compounds called silicates. Boric oxide is added to the glass recipe to make special borosilicate glass.

Borosilicate glasses were first made around 1890, in Germany. When they are heated, they expand much less than ordinary glass, making them less likely to crack. The best known variety today is called Pyrex. This contains about 15 percent boric oxide. Pyrex is used mainly to make see-through jugs and dishes that do not melt or crack when heated.

Borosilicate glass is also strong. It is used as glass fiber. Glass fibers are molded to make lightweight but strong structures, such as small boats or gliders (airplanes without engines). Glass wool used for insulation is also made with borosilicates.

Glass made of pure borate compounds also exists. This breaks very easily, but it is sometimes used to make camera lenses.

Borates are used to make enamel. This is the thin glassy coating used to cover metal objects, such as pans and cooktops. Potters use boric oxide as an ingredient of glazes (the protective coatings on pottery).

Some boron compounds, such as metal borides, are types of ceramic. Ceramics are pottery-like substances. They are resistant to heat and have high melting points. This makes borides useful under extreme conditions. For example, they are used to make containers for handling melted

*A plane drops powdered boron compounds on to a burning forest in California. The powder smothers the flames. The boron compounds also coat the tree trunks and branches. This makes the wood fireproof and protects the trees from the flames.*

aluminum. The hexagonal form of boron nitride is also useful for insulating things against both heat and electricity.

Boric acid is used to fireproof objects. It is particularly good for making wood and paper resistant to fire. During wild fires, firefighters drop boric acid onto the flames.

## The nuclear industry

Nuclear reactors in power plants obtain energy from the breakup of radioactive atoms, especially atoms of the heavy metals uranium and thorium. Radioactive atoms are so unstable that their nucleus splits into two smaller atoms. This process is called nuclear fission—or splitting the atom. Fission releases a lot of heat and neutrons that travel through the reactor.

Eventually the neutrons hit another uranium atom. This triggers another fission reaction and releases more heat. Soon many fission reactions are happening all at once throughout the reactor. This is called a chain reaction because each fission produces many more.

It is important to control the number of neutrons in the reactor to make sure that the chain reaction does not run so fast that it produces a nuclear explosion. The isotope boron-10 is very good at absorbing neutrons. Since the beginning of the nuclear power industry, boron-10 has been used in control rods that are lowered into a reactor to slow the fission reactions.

## ATOMS AT WORK

Atoms of boron-10 are used to absorb neutrons produced by nuclear fission. This is a nuclear reaction, not a chemical one because it involves the nucleus of the atom rather than the outer electrons. A neutron, produced by a uranium atom splitting in two, travels through the nuclear reactor. If it hits a boron-10 atom, the neutron will be absorbed by the atom.

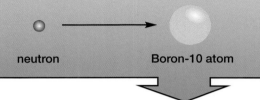

neutron        Boron-10 atom

When the neutron hits the boron atom it causes the atom to divide into two making a lithium atom and an alpha particle. An alpha particle is made of two protons and two neutrons. It has a positive charge.

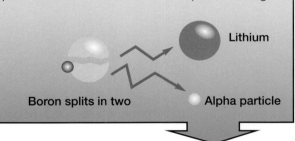

Lithium

Boron splits in two       Alpha particle

The alpha particle picks up two electrons from other atoms nearby and becomes a helium atom.

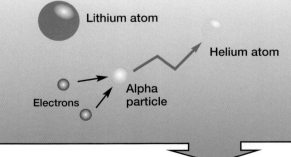

Lithium atom

Helium atom

Electrons      Alpha particle

The reaction that takes place can be written like this:

**B-10 + neutron → Li + He**

*Powdered boron is mixed with explosives to produce the green color in fireworks.*

To make the rods, boron that is high in boron-10 has to be prepared by a complicated separation process. It is then made into powdered boron carbide and packed into hollow rods. Boric acid in the cooling water around reactors also helps to stop neutrons from escaping.

## Cleaning products

Borax was first added to soap in the late 1800s to make the soap better at washing clothes. From about 1907, the compound sodium perborate began to be used as bleach. Today, borates are also part of many household washing powders and liquids. They help to control the acidity of the wash and loosen dirt particles. Borates are also good antiseptics (substances that kill germs).

## Other uses

Boron and its compounds have many other uses. In the electronics industry, boron is used in semiconductors. These are substances, such as silicon, that have useful electrical properties, and are used in electronic equipment. Small amounts of boron are added to silicon to change the way it conducts electricity.

Amorphous boron is often used in fireworks and flares, where it gives off a green light. Other industries that use boron compounds include leather, paper, and explosive manufacturers.

# Strength and hardness

The modern world depends on tough, high-performance materials. Boron and its compounds are now used widely in industries where extreme hardness and strength is required.

## As hard as diamonds

Very hard materials such as boron carbide and boron nitride are useful in two main situations: to make objects that will not wear away easily or to make grinders and cutters that slice through other substances.

Boron carbide was first made in the nineteenth century, although it was not used in industry until much later. Scientists at the time hoped that it would become a useful abrasive (a hard substance used for grinding). Small crystals of boron carbide can be attached to the rims of grinding wheels and used to cut stone and metal. Unfortunately, rubbing against the stone or metal as it cuts makes the carbide very hot, and it reacts with the materials it is cutting. For this reasons, boron carbide is now only used as a loose abrasive powder, to polish precious stones, for example.

Powdered boron carbide can also be heated and pressed into shapes. In this form it is used in wear-resistant machinery, nozzles for sandblasting equipment, and for military armor, including body armor.

*A factory worker lifts a block of cermet out of a furnace. Cermet is a mixture of boron carbide and aluminum. When it has cooled the block will be very light but stronger than steel.*

A hard form of boron nitride was first manufactured in 1957 under the name Borazon. The equipment used to make this material was also used to make artificial diamonds. Although it costs more than boron carbide, boron nitride is very good for cutting through steel and other metals. It can also cut at high temperatures.

23

## Boron fibers

A lump of pure boron is very strong, but brittle. Thin fibers made of pure boron are more flexible. When the fibers are embedded in another material, such as plastic or aluminum, they make an extremely light but tough material.

Boron fibers were first developed in the 1960s in the United States, and were much stiffer than things made from glass fibers. At first, there was great excitement that boron could be used to make all kinds of products. However, boron was too expensive to replace most glass-fiber objects. Nevertheless, boron-fiber materials are used in space shuttles and some military aircraft. They are even used to make golf clubs.

One reason boron fibers have not been more successful is because of carbon fibers. These carbon fibers work in a similar way, but are much easier to make. Making boron fibers is a complex process involving the dangerous gas boron trichloride. Pure boron is made by reacting this gas at high temperatures. The boron is then cooled

*Boron compounds are used in the tough enamel that coats cooking pots. The hard enamel protects the pot from damage and helps it heat up evenly.*

*A gear wheel is hardened by "boronizing." The wheel is heated in sand mixed with boron gas.*

until it forms solid fibers. These are wound around very thin wires of another material, such as tungsten metal.

## Changing metals

Boron is added to metals in small amounts to make alloys. (An alloy is a metal containing one metallic element mixed with atoms of other elements.) For example, an iron–boron alloy called ferroboron is added to steel to make it harder. Some boron is also added to copper and aluminum when they are being refined to help get rid of impurities. Alloys used to make magnets often contain boron, too.

Engineers can make the surface of a metal very hard by "boronizing" it. The metal is heated in boron gas. The boron atoms coat the surface of the metal, forming a hard coating of metal boride.

### DID YOU KNOW?

Material science is the study of how materials bend and break. In material science, hardness and strength are not the same thing. One substance is harder than another if the first can scratch the second but the second substance cannot scratch the first. Strength is a more difficult concept. If a substance can be pulled and squashed without breaking, it is strong. However, strong substances can be brittle (crack easily) or tough (resist cracking). Finally, substances can either be flexible (bend easily) or stiff (resist bending).

# Boron and living things

In small amounts, boron is essential to most types of life. Plants need it to grow properly. Without plants, there would be no animals, including humans. Boron is also used in medicines. Borax has been used for centuries in lotions, and today boron has a role in treating cancer.

### The essential element

Most soils contain boron minerals. Most of these are dissolved in water as boric acid. Plants absorb boric acid and other minerals when they take in water through their roots. Plants use the boron to keep their leaves and stems strong. Plants cells have thick walls made of sugar-based compounds. Scientists have shown that 90 percent of the boron taken up by a plant goes into building these cell walls. The walls make the plant strong but also flexible.

In some places, such as parts of China and Iran, there is not enough boron in the soil. Crops growing without boron suffer in various ways. For example, celery does not

*Grapes are a good source of boron minerals. Other foods rich in boron-containing compounds include nuts, prunes, and peas.*

*Bandages and medical dressings used to cover wounds and cuts are coated in boric acid. Boric acid is a very mild antiseptic. It keeps the cut clean without stopping the healing process.*

grow straight, and peanuts may be hollow in the middle. To help plants grow better many farms have to be treated with boron-containing fertilizers.

## DID YOU KNOW?

### *TARGETING CANCER*

When body cells begin to grow uncontrollably, they produce a cancer. As the cancer grows it damages healthy parts of the body. Eventually the cancer will cause the person to die. Boron-10 atoms are now used in a cancer therapy called "boron neutron capture therapy" (BNCT). A cancer sufferer is first given drugs that contain boron-10 atoms. Cancer cells absorb these atoms. Doctors then aim a beam of neutrons at the cancer from outside the body. The boron-10 atoms absorb the neutrons, like they do in a nuclear reactor. This causes the boron atoms to split up and kill the cancer cells. BNCT is sometimes used on cancers that are deep inside the brain and difficult to treat in any other way.

Animals (including humans) also need boron in very tiny amounts. Boron is used by many parts of the body. People who do not have enough boron in their food may have difficulty having babies and have other problems. However, the body needs less than 10 milligrams of boron a day—there are 28,350 milligrams in 1 ounce. There is plenty of boron in a well-rounded diet.

## Healthy poison

Too much boron can poison plants, too, and some boron compounds are used as weedkillers (as well as fertilizers). Boric acid is now widely used as a pesticide (a substance that kills insects and other pests). Scattered as a fine powder down cracks and beneath floorboards, it controls cockroaches and other insects. It is safer for people to use boric acid in their homes than more powerful pesticides.

# Periodic table

Everything in the universe is made from combinations of substances called elements. Elements are made of tiny atoms, which are too small to see. Atoms are the building blocks of matter.

The character of an atom depends on how many even tinier particles called protons there are in its center, or nucleus. An element's atomic number is the same as the number of its protons.

Scientists have found around 116 different elements. About 90 elements occur naturally on Earth. The rest have been made in experiments.

All these elements are set out on a chart called the periodic table. This lists all the elements in order according to their atomic number.

The elements at the left of the table are metals. Those at the right are nonmetals. Between the metals and the nonmetals are the metalloids, which sometimes act like metals and sometimes like nonmetals.

- On the left of the table are the alkali metals. These have just one outer electron.

- Metals get more reactive as you go down a group. The most reactive nonmetals are at the top of the table.

- On the right of the periodic table are the noble gases. These elements have full outer shells.

- The number of electrons orbiting the nucleus increases down each group.

- Elements in the same group have the same number of electrons in their outer shells.

- The transition metals are in the middle of the table, between Groups II and III.

**Group I**

| 1 |
|---|
| H |
| Hydrogen |
| 1 |

**Group II**

**Transition metals**

| 3 | 4 |
|---|---|
| Li | Be |
| Lithium | Beryllium |
| 7 | 9 |

| 11 | 12 |
|---|---|
| Na | Mg |
| Sodium | Magnesium |
| 23 | 24 |

| 19 | 20 | 21 | 22 | 23 | 24 | 25 | 26 | 27 |
|---|---|---|---|---|---|---|---|---|
| K | Ca | Sc | Ti | V | Cr | Mn | Fe | Co |
| Potassium | Calcium | Scandium | Titanium | Vanadium | Chromium | Manganese | Iron | Cobalt |
| 39 | 40 | 45 | 48 | 51 | 52 | 55 | 56 | 59 |
| 37 | 38 | 39 | 40 | 41 | 42 | 43 | 44 | 45 |
| Rb | Sr | Y | Zr | Nb | Mo | Tc | Ru | Rh |
| Rubidium | Strontium | Yttrium | Zirconium | Niobium | Molybdenum | Technetium | Ruthenium | Rhodium |
| 85 | 88 | 89 | 91 | 93 | 96 | (98) | 101 | 103 |
| 55 | 56 | 71 | 72 | 73 | 74 | 75 | 76 | 77 |
| Cs | Ba | Lu | Hf | Ta | W | Re | Os | Ir |
| Cesium | Barium | Lutetium | Hafnium | Tantalum | Tungsten | Rhenium | Osmium | Iridium |
| 133 | 137 | 175 | 179 | 181 | 184 | 186 | 190 | 192 |
| 87 | 88 | 103 | 104 | 105 | 106 | 107 | 108 | 109 |
| Fr | Ra | Lr | Rf | Db | Sg | Bh | Hs | Mt |
| Francium | Radium | Lawrencium | Rutherfordium | Dubnium | Seaborgium | Bohrium | Hassium | Meitnerium |
| 223 | 226 | (260) | (263) | (268) | (266) | (272) | (277) | (276) |

**Lanthanide elements**

**Actinide elements**

| 57 | 58 | 59 | 60 | 61 |
|---|---|---|---|---|
| La | Ce | Pr | Nd | Pm |
| Lanthanum | Cerium | Praseodymium | Neodymium | Promethium |
| 39 | 140 | 141 | 144 | (145) |
| 89 | 90 | 91 | 92 | 93 |
| Ac | Th | Pa | U | Np |
| Actinium | Thorium | Protactinium | Uranium | Neptunium |
| 227 | 232 | 231 | 238 | (237) |

The horizontal rows are called periods. As you go across a period, the atomic number increases by one from each element to the next. The vertical columns are called groups. Elements get heavier as you go down a group. All the elements in a group have the same number of electrons in their outer shells. This means they react in similar ways.

The transition metals fall between Groups II and III. Their electron shells fill up in an unusual way. The lanthanide elements and the actinide elements are set apart from the main table to make it easier to read. All the lanthanide elements and the actinide elements are quite rare.

## Boron in the table

Boron is in group III of the periodic table. It is a metalloid, since it shares properties with both metals and nonmetals. Boron has three electrons in its outer shell. This makes it unreactive compared to most elements. However, when it does react with other elements, boron forms a huge variety of different compounds.

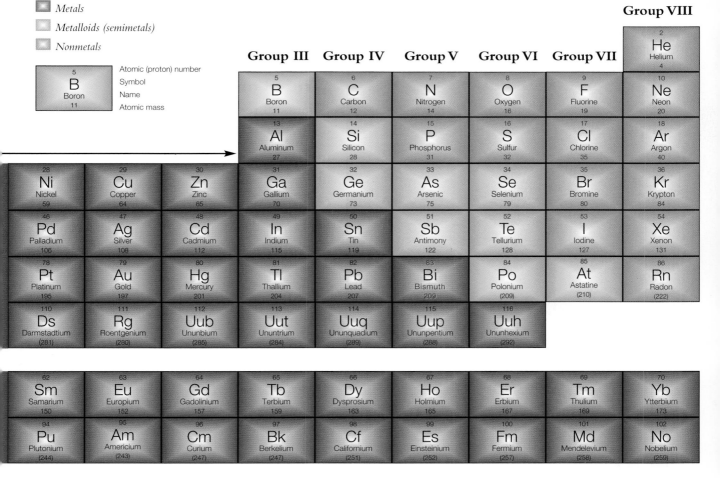

# Chemical reactions

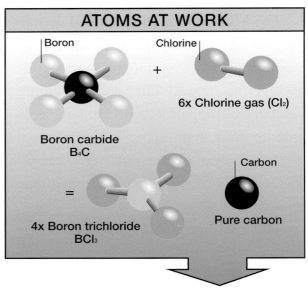

**ATOMS AT WORK**

Boron

Chlorine

+

6x Chlorine gas (Cl₂)

Boron carbide
B₄C

Carbon

=

Pure carbon

4x Boron trichloride
BCl₃

hemical reactions are going on around us all the time. Some reactions involve just two substances; others many more. But whenever a reaction takes place, at least one substance is changed.

In a chemical reaction, the number of atoms stays the same. But they join up in different combinations.

The reaction that takes place when boron carbide reacts with chlorine is written like this:

$$B_4C + 6Cl_2 \rightarrow C + 4BCl_3$$

*Boron-containing compounds are used in many cleaning products. The boron compounds help to break up dirt.*

## Writing an equation

Chemical reactions can be described by writing down the number of atoms and molecules before the reaction and the atoms and molecules after the reaction. Chemists write the reaction as an equation. This shows what happens in the chemical reaction.

## Making it balance

When the numbers of each atom on both sides of the equation are equal, the equation is balanced. If the numbers are not equal, something is wrong. The chemist must adjust the number of atoms involved until the equation balances.

# Glossary

**acid:** An acid is a chemical that releases hydrogen ions easily during reactions.

**amorphous:** When a substance does not have an obvious repeating crystal structure, so it is found in several shapes.

**atom:** The smallest part of an element having all the properties of that element. Each atom is less than a millionth of an inch in diameter.

**atomic mass number:** The number of protons and neutrons in an atom.

**atomic number:** The number of protons in the nucleus of an atom.

**bond:** The attraction between two atoms, or ions, that holds them together.

**compound:** A new substance made when two or more elements chemically join together.

**crystal:** A solid consisting of a repeating pattern of atoms, ions, or molecules.

**electron:** A tiny particle with a negative charge. Electrons are found inside atoms, where they move around the nucleus in layers called electron shells.

**element:** A substance that is made from only one type of atom.

**ion:** An atom or a group of atoms that has lost or gained electrons to become electrically charged.

**mineral:** A compound or element as it is found in its natural form in Earth.

**neutron:** A tiny particle with no electrical charge. Neutrons are found in the nucleus of almost every atom.

**nuclear fission:** A type of nuclear reaction that involves one atom splitting up into two smaller units.

**nuclear reaction:** When atoms change from one element into another. This can be because the atom has split into two smaller units, or it could be caused by two atoms fusing together to make a larger atom.

**nuclear reactor:** A machine that controls a nuclear reaction happening inside it.

**nucleus:** The dense structure at the center of an atom. Protons and neutrons are found inside the nucleus of an atom.

**ore:** A mineral or rock that contains enough of a particular substance to make it useful for mining.

**periodic table:** A chart of all the chemical elements laid out in order of their atomic number.

**proton:** A tiny particle with a positive charge. Protons are found inside the nucleus of an atom.

**radioactivity:** The release of energy and radiation caused by an atom's nucleus breaking apart. This also causes changes to the number of particles in the nucleus.

**reaction:** A process in which two or more elements or compounds combine to produce new substances.

**solution:** A liquid that has another substance dissolved in it.

# Index